FINISHING LINE PRESS

www.finishinglinepress.com

For Father
and Many Other Things

poems by

Matthew Diomede, Ph.D.

Finishing Line Press
Georgetown, Kentucky

For Father
and Many Other Things

ACKNOWLEDGMENTS

I appreciate Roy Peter Clark's support. I thank John Ashbery for choosing this
manuscript as an Award Finalist in the Virginia Commonwealth University
Contemporary Poetry Series. I thank Dr. Al Montesi, Dr. Melvin Backman
and David Petteys for their encouragement.

Publisher: Leah Huete de Maines
Editor: Christen Kincaid
Cover Art: Matthew Diomede, Ph.D.
Author Photo: Matthew Diomede, Ph.D.
Cover Design: Elizabeth Maines McCleavy

Order online: www.finishinglinepress.com

Author inquiries and mail orders:
Finishing Line Press
P. O. Box 1626
Georgetown, Kentucky 40324
U. S. A.

Table of Contents

For my Italian father and mother,
my wife Barbara
and my whole Italian-American family
and all of nature

Stabbing

in the cave
of primitive
thought
I found
a piece of darkness

I shaped it
into a point
and called it
light

A Morning Prayer

This day I dedicate to you,
Father.
Each breath I breathe will
remind me of your laughter,
your temper, your hope,
and your love.

Prayer to Mother

mother flower,
take a sun
and call it freedom
bend its petals open,
casting your morning
seed to the wind
that wants to play folly
and let loose a day

Splitting

night father
split
my day mother
into
the life of
a son
that found
a day father
and a night mother
first came youth of the son
then came middle age
awaiting old age,
he loves both father and mother

Father

In my father's hands
are the cuts and wounds
of his work he so
carefully painted with iodine,
never liking to talk about them.
He carries them
like his past
I know nothing about.

At the Beach

I have found my mother's anger and my father's carelessness,
laid them like clams on a hard, heavy
white-capped sea rock and smashed them,
pieces of shells holding white sunshine.
Nearby a tern with typing feet
printed on the cold, fresh, concrete sand
who I was.

In Search of a Past

I thought I saw
them bringing my
body into my
grandfather's field;
they carry my mind
to my grandmother.
I have not seen them
and do not know them,
yet they are with me,
holding Father in my heart.

Back Then

Grandfather and grandmother of my father,
whom I never even saw,
who were you that
brought him to
me? You, both,
in my mind,
like my dreams
trying to live.
I know who you are.

sun-search

mother sunset
seeks her
son, wandering
into darkness,
chirping like mad birds
looking for their fathers

Transformation-Enclosure

I live at my mother's breast,
sucking yesterday's vinegar
and tomorrow's wine,
nurtured by my father's
persistence.
In the fetal position,
I return to a primitive past
where I see
white doves circling
my grave;
they drop minutes and hours on my coffin,
they give me time
to find my escape

Mother Images

 I have come out of the ground
and what I see is my mother's scalp
hanging from the sunrise
while my father plays the banjo.
Starlings a few feet from me
are about to attack.
I will crawl into the thirty-third sphere,
and Beatrice will whisper to me tales of my
mother,
I, blind to myself, forgot to see light
in the darkness of Hades.

Poem after Kafka's "Letter to His Father"

"Life is more than a Chinese puzzle."
F. Kafka

The time I came home,
with my khaki duffle bag,
from Marine Officer Training
and failed, you father, were
laying cinder blocks for our summer bungalow foundation.
I dropped my bag, and sadly told you. "I did my best,"
and you got angry and continued to work.
You took a piece of the foundation out that day.

Father

Father, my wife and I came to get you
in our sailboat.
You stood shivering in the water, your skin blue,
your eyes like a man about to die. I swam back
to get your clothes you left on shore.
We placed an orange preserver and a woolen
shirt on you as you shivered.
We took you back to shore. The week
before you argued with Mom. You knew you were
out too long and too far, up to your neck in
it, not knowing how to swim, and pushing
yourself to do the things you have to
I will not forget how far you went.

A Father's Message

He looked into the rectangular box,
lying strong like a living poplar in New England,
his mind scanning his old basement steps
where his father did all sorts of things:
collected junk, read his magazines, posted his pin-up girls, marked
    his many calendars,
collected discount coupons, worked infinitely
with his tools in his silent escape.
His eyes sealed against the darkness
carry in them no escape but all that he was.
From the side, I hear my Italian mother
weeping, calling me.
I will tell what we both know.

Poem at the Beach

Glory be to the
drowned boy
I saw the them
try to revive in my youth.
His thin, black denim trousers,
his beach blanket,
his single record album,
were the only things the lifeguards
found that day.
He was poor, and we could all tell,
as we watched.
He will come into my mind
when I become a Father:
praise his thin white arms;
they are the arms of a son.
Then I heard the lifeguards vomiting.

Where Real Tears Are

Flower talked to
sun.
Sun spoke to
mountain.
Sky thundered
snow.
Out of the forest
came a rabbit sniffling real hard.

Seasonal Question

The trees,
why do they stand still
in autumn rain,
gazing out like
hypnotized dogs
whose eyes look into fire?

Autumn Dream

The leaves,
they are dead,
they peer out
of frozen trees
with large dazed eyes.

Images

Fallen leaves of pear
lie frozen and curled black
like smiling wrinkles of
a dead, old woman's face.

Death

brown skeleton
of a painted leaf
on a
white garage door
you tried to
get in during
last night's storm
you stand like a ghost
trying to find
an entrance to some desperate home
tomorrow
they will lift and
lower you
like faithful undertakers

I am dead now

I am dead now
the stones are my eyes
the dark mountain is my brain
my ears are the dead hawks
my nose is a frozen stream
my mouth is sealed like
snow that covers all I see
suddenly a crocus pushes through

Into Another World

The flies are dead today
waiting to be swept off
some dusty windowsill.
they think they will
fall into another world—
a transmigration—they
lie like Egyptian mummies,
some taped up in strips of
brown soil.

Seasonal Function

The crew-cut winter
forest bares its head
to the winter gray sky
who taps
him with a cold, white hand.

Envelope

On a white morning
the bird bath lies frozen,
holding frost
that seals
what I saw a warm
sun open.

skulls

the snow
shuts
in
your ground thoughts
and you wait for them
to break out of this blanketed brain
that hides on winter days and nights
suddenly your black skull
peaks through a white hole
the squirrels come to drink
and your brain tries to cover
itself with a patch of snow

The Fireman

The fog
climbs a mountain
ladder, exiting at
our chalet, trying
to break through our
glass door.
Moments later
it calls for help—
they keep climbing,
thinking there's some
fire within.

Inner Structure

The creaking of the beam of
the house on this windy day
gnaws at me,
some inner
emotion that
is shaking
the house,
asking itself
if it has enough nails
or if the nails
have not rusted.
Some primitive hammer
keeps telling us that
it made its imprint
long ago.

Still-Born

Hate is a blind
hawk bearing
children that cannot ever
fly into a sun
that falls short
never touching the
cold mountain ledge
that carries
a dead nest
in her womb.

Feeling the Earth and the Insects

The birds have come to
die today. They bring
their wings to the
bird bath, spreading
them out, cleansing all
on their old sins. They lie
on the surface like
St. Peter wishing they
had wings that could take them
to another heaven.

The Center

The conversation I hold with
myself is like the spider
that knits its target, the thin threads
spreading out from inner zones
into outer perimeters, starting with 1000 points,
moving to 200.
In the center a fly
who whispers to himself
perimeters he thought
he would never cross.

Reinforcement

The spider builds its
web, the wired
thread hangs in
some empty corner,
trying to hold up
cracked plaster.

Conversations

We are all talking
to humans
that sound like
houses that creak in
windy weather.
In some the creaking lasts longer,
the pronouncing
hesitantly stuttering
some inner messages
that beams are made for.

night morgue

nightmare
strangles our heart
and it bleeds
drops of fear
until our blood
is all out of us
and we are dead
the waking is the
breathing

Windows

wind squeezes
through aluminum
storm windows
in winter,
slicing into a mind
that looks out,
trying to stop
hasty invaders
the putty we all use
will not hold

Accompaniment

Rain always knows
when it comes.
It lets you talk,
then joins in,
two voices merging
into a loud flood.

Interment

When the loggers
felled the trees
on a moon-lit funeral night,
we tipped-toed
from thick woods,
whispering prayers
to an open sky.

On Awakening

The
dog
that came
barking
snow
into
my dreams
rushed
into
a
melting
sun.

Planting

Will I, like
the conifers
that drop
their spiraled children,
lie under the
tree of night,
gazing at smiling
stars, or will I
enter the earth,
bearing a tree I never knew?

Escape

White rose
climbs under eaves,
still intact;
its sisters lie rusted
in gold, autumn morning sun.

Hastening

When the junco
returns,
he brings
his gray winter
coat;
pressed white is his breast
like
spring
rushing
in.

Revenge

I have pulled
a sky
and stretched it
across the ground,
burying it with dirt.
At night I thought
I saw stars peek through.

Summer Sunset

My eyes drown in
red white streams
that run through
huge blue forests
while
snow
swims with its thin arms
and legs into the sun.

Tossing Turtles

He took a turn
at tossing turtles in his mind.
Their heads peep frantically
out of his eyes
in and old, hard, skin face
wrinkled into tiny creases of time
holding mysteries of old turtle shells.

Protestations

Gold leaves shake in
autumn air, protesting their graves.
A few will hang
all winter
like stars on a black night.

Creation

Between the lines of
my poem,
a baby spider runs
trying to race
out of it.
It runs quickly
past my theme, my conclusion
and meets its end
under my finger.

Father

This person I call father,
I keep casting off.
The older I get
the closer we become.

Dr. Matthew Diomede teaches English/Writing at the University of Tampa. He has taught at the University of South Florida, St. Louis University, University of Missouri, and other universities. He has taught literary criticism, literature, vocabulary, composition/advanced writing, creative writing and other courses. His undergraduate degree is from Fordham University where he received a track athletic scholarship. He has two masters degrees from Fordham and Long Island University. His Ph.D. in English is from St. Louis University. His revised Ph.D. dissertation on an Italian-American writer was published by Bucknell University Press: *Pietro DiDonato, the Master Builder.* Two chapters from this book have been reprinted in *Twentieth Century Criticism* (TCLC) and reproduced in *Literature Resource Center.* He has published over 100 poems, prose, and fiction and has received several writing awards. He is listed in *A Directory of American Poets.* He served in the U.S. Marine Corps Reserve for six years.